ASPEN SPECIAL EDITION

Text by Bob Diddlebock
Photography by David Lissy

Aspen: The Mountains

Fate has smiled on the Roaring Fork River Valley, lavishing it with the sheer slopes, powdery snow and sunshine that make skiing such an earthly delight for up to seven months a year.

Little wonder that Aspen holds the unique distinction of having four world-class mountains that challenge everyone from the raw beginner to the most seasoned pro.

There's steep, deep and chic Aspen Mountain, a stone's throw from the downtown mall. There's Aspen Highlands, a favorite with the locals who enjoy the laid-back, "Howdy, partner" hospitality. There's Buttermilk, ideal for rubbery-legged beginners. And then there's mammoth Snowmass, with its ski-in, ski-out access and variety of runs that families love.

Aspen

In this oh-so-trendy town of 5,500 year-round residents, skiing is big business, having grown from two trails and two chair lifts on Aspen Mountain in the 1940s to a billion-dollar industry. Today, the extent of that success is such that there's now talk of building a high-speed tramway that could transport up to 2,500 passengers an hour from downtown Aspen to Snowmass at speeds of up to 30 miles an hour.

Aspen Mountain, which towers over the town, is a mecca for serious skiers, as well as celebrity watchers who can occasionally catch mega-stars like Jack Nicholson navigating the slopes. Dubbed "America's Mountain," it has some 75 trails well laid out over 625 acres, the place you head for a long day of tough, hard skiing. Little wonder that with a vertical drop of more than 3,200 feet, the experts call it a "fun mountain."

Walshs Gulch, a double black diamond run, is as steep as you'll find in Aspen, and if you can conquer that, you might as well be on the pro tour. The longest run — which covers the 1 & 2 Leaf, Northstar, Gentlemans Ridge and Little Nell — goes on for three miles.

Ironically, the toughest terrain is toward the bottom, with the intermediate runs laid out at the top. But with the addition of the Silver Queen Gondola, less-than-expert skiers can now get up to the summit in just 13 minutes.

Of course, one key to successfully skiing Aspen Mountain is keeping your radar on because it's always crowded. But that's one of its charms, because you never know *who* you might run into....

Aspen Highlands

The star of the show at Aspen Highlands, along with its 3,800-foot vertical drop, is the scenery, which is perhaps the most spectacular in the Rockies thanks to heart-stopping views of the Maroon Bells wilderness area.

A favorite among the locals who fondly refer to it as Aspen's "other" mountain, Highlands doesn't have gondolas and doesn't draw the Hollywood crowd; instead of Gucci snowsuits, you're more likely to see blue jeans and cowboy hats. Highlands' stock in trade is its down-home attitude and no-frills skiing suited for good intermediates.

If Aspen gets an overnight snowfall, your best bet for some fun powder skiing is Highlands' Olympic Bowl, with its 800-foot drop that's made for aggressive intermediates and experts. Another black slope, Steeplechase, is a roller coaster ride straight down that can push the best skiers, which also holds true for the Moment of Truth trail. Then there's Scarlett Run, a tough blue slope with bumps that'll make you feel like Billy Kidd if you get through it in one piece.

i

COLORADO

Buttermilk

Southwest of town on Highway 82 in the shadow of the Maroon Bells is where you'll find Buttermilk Mountain with its wide, gentle slopes and rolling knolls that wind through the White River National Forest. It combines gentle beginner runs and easy intermediate trails, while holding a few hidden secrets the locals try to keep to themselves.

Legend has it the mountain got its name in the late 1800s from town maidens who'd lug buckets of milk up to the railroad crewmen, or "tiehacks," who were cutting down trees for railroad ties. The maidens' trips sometimes took so long that by the time they reached the men, their once-fresh milk had soured.

Aspen legend Friedl Pfeifer opened the ski area in 1958 because, as manager Bill Beyer put it at the time, "Skiing is no longer a sport for the exclusive set. It has become an activity for the whole family."

The longest run is three miles and there are no expert slopes, but the Tiehack side of the mountain features moguls, glades, steeper slopes and powder. It's a good place to learn how to use telemark, or cross-country skis, on a downhill slope. And when there's a storm, more than a few local residents come out to enjoy the deep powder that forms in so many of the aspen and spruce groves.

Snowmass

The contrasts between the town of Aspen and the Snowmass resort are striking.

Aspen's Victorian charm harks back to the days when the village was a wild mining camp with a few civilized graces. Snowmass, in contrast, is a contemporary village that offers ski-in, ski-out convenience from its slope-side lodges, condominiums and private homes. It's ideal for families and groups who want to ski, eat and shop without going too far out of their way. And for the non-skier, there's the Snowmass Repertory Theatre and the Anderson Ranch Arts Center, which offers first-class workshops on ceramics, photography and wood-working.

Snowmass was built on Baldy Mountain in the mid-1960s, when planned, self-contained communities were the rage in American architectural circles. Developer and ski enthusiast Bill Janss and his aides used computers to map ski trails, lift routes and building sites for homes and condos. When it was completed, the resort was ballyhooed as the "exciting new Shangri-la of skiing" and as another "instant resort," much like Vail.

The mountain, which is so big that some schussers have been known to get lost on it, offers a great variety of skiing: steep and deep, through the trees, or nice and easy. There are virtually no lift lines, and it's easy to escape the crowds that can sometimes make skiing on other mountains a kamikaze exercise.

Beginners can get started on Fanny Hill and Assay Hill. The mile-wide and mile-and-a-half-long Big Burn is for intermediates and meanders through copses of evergreen trees. Garret Gulch and the Hanging Valley Wall are for experts, and up top at almost 12,000 feet, there's expert bowl skiing in the Cirque.

A high-speed quad "superchair" was installed in 1987 that can ferry 2,800 skiers an hour to the mountain's top, a trip that takes only eight minutes and provides access to runs guaranteed to please every member of the family. **

iii

Snowmass Mountain rises behind the Sam's Knob area, Snowmass

COLORADO

World Cup Week, or Winternational as it's known in these parts, is when all Aspen shines ... and parties ... and has fun ... and, oh yes, does a little skiing, too.

As one local has described it, Aspen becomes something of a Camelot with snow frosting, a town that forsakes its western roots and takes on more of an international, European flavor.

Celebrities, VIPs and heavy hitters from the world over dance at Andre's, eat at Gordon's, attend black tie balls, and cheer on the world's best professional skiers as they try to tame Aspen Mountain's fast runs.

Part of the World Cup's appeal in Aspen is the fact that racegoers can usually find the skiers mingling in town, which is a break from most tour stops where the athletes generally stay cloistered in their rooms and eat in dormitories.

"Throughout the week, there's this feeling not of great competition, but of relaxed competition," says one race organizer. "When the skiers come to Aspen, I think they come to have fun."

Monika Maierhofer of Austria descends a tough slalom course, Aspen

Whether the women or the men hold center stage, the racers face one of the most challenging runs on the World Cup's North American leg. Aspen Mountain's two-mile-long downhill course, with its 2,600-foot vertical drop, has created its share of memorable moments.

Take 1981, for instance, when a snow drought forced race organizers to make their own snow for days, as well as to truck it in from other mountains. Then, on the day of the race, it snowed so hard that competition had to be postponed.

Race chief Tom Anderson recalls the time in 1984 when Billy Johnson — who'd just won the gold medal in the men's downhill at the Winter Olympics in Sarajevo — said to him, "This is the best course I've skied on; you guys have done a fabulous job. I'm gonna win this ...."

Of course, Johnson, who always liked Colorado's soft, fresh snow, went out and beat the goggles off everyone.

Indeed, Aspen has one of Colorado's more illustrious skiing histories.

The sport first began to take wing during the gold and silver rush days of the late 1800s, when miners strapped handmade boards — some of them up to 12 feet long — to their feet to get from camp to camp and claim to claim.

Aspen's first ski run was built on Aspen Mountain, then known as Ajax, in the late 1930s by Andre Roch, who also formed the Aspen Ski Club. International races were held on Ajax in 1941 under Roch's sponsorship, but not much else happened during the World War II years.

When Walter Paepcke, who helped build Aspen into the recreational mecca it is today, appeared on the scene, things began to change.

After building more sophisticated runs on Aspen Mountain, Paepcke and his skiing aide de camp, Friedl Pfeifer, brought the 1950 International Ski Federation championships to

an event that put the obscure village on the international ski map.

The Buttermilk ski mountain made headlines when it hosted the world's first professional ski race in January 1961, a mile-long giant slalom event with 16 gates won by Christian Pravda, an Austrian native and Sun Valley instructor. His take: $1,500.

In 1978, the World Cup came to town. Three years later, Subaru joined the Aspen Skiing Company to create the Subaru Aspen Winternational, and in the course of eight years, the event has grown from a three-day event to a weeklong celebration.

The men's downhill begins at the top of Aspen Mountain on Ruthies Run and cuts into the Aztec stretch where racers approach speeds of up to 70 miles an hour. From there, it's on to Spring Pitch. After a tight technical turn, the racers hit the Dago Cut Road, pick up more speed and hit the course's most technical stretch by the Strawpile. From there, it's a row of bumps onto the slick Norway run and into a fast finish by Lift 1A at the Shadow Mountain condo complex.

Racers who can ride a flat ski while gliding and then ride the edges well — and racers who can respond to a lot of changes in the course — do well. The rule of thumb is "Don't relax or you're dead."

As race chief Anderson says, "We take a lot of pride in putting on a good race, and many tell us that we do a better job than many of the Europeans."

That's quite a statement, but then again, this is Aspen, where anything less than the best just isn't worth doing.

COLORADO Ski!

In just over 40 years, Aspen has grown from a sleepy town that time had all but forgotten to one of the world's most popular ski resorts, a transformation that has left old-timers shaking their heads and newcomers asking, "What's next?"

Tucked high in the Rockies at 7,900 feet, Aspen is a town of 5,500 year-round residents, as well as thousands of seasonal visitors who

A horse and buggy await skiers and mall shoppers, Aspen

consider themselves quite lucky. After all, where else can you find the mountains, the arts, the recreational opportunities and, of course, winter's deep snows conspiring to create what many believe is the ideal lifestyle?

It hasn't always been this way. Indeed, it's hard to imagine the town's rough-and-tumble birth when silver-hungry miners from the boom town of Leadville spilled over Independence Pass into the glacier-carved Roaring Fork River Valley in 1879, chasing out the Ute Indians and setting up camp at the foot of Aspen Mountain.

At first, the town numbered 35 residents. By early 1884, thanks to several multi-million-dollar silver strikes, the population had risen to 2,500. At the end of the year, the town numbered 5,000 residents, with more streaming in as news of the valley's riches spread to Denver and points farther east.

With that, schools, churches, a fire department, hotels, an opera house, three banks, six newspapers, a water system, a hydroelectric plant, several bordellos and a racetrack were built. As one writer put it at the time, "Aspen is the handsomest and most substantial town in the Rockies."

The hub of downtown activity was, as it is today, the Jerome Hotel, whose owner, Jerome

Wheeler, had been the president of Macy's in New York before heading west to sink $6 million into several Aspen ventures, including the town's first bank.

In short time, his Jerome was the Rockies' best hotel, with its pulley-operated elevators, electric lights, plush furnishings, hot and cold running water, guest-paging system, Parisian chef and German horticulturist.

As the 1880s drew to a close, Pitkin County mines were producing $10 million worth of ore a year, which was being shipped over the mountains on the Denver and Rio Grande Railroad line. By 1892, Aspen's population topped 11,000 — making it Colorado's third largest town behind Denver and Leadville — and life couldn't have been better.

But all that ended when the United States went to the gold standard for its currency in 1893, a turn that sent silver prices crashing faster than a runaway ore train. Within weeks, Aspen was all but deserted, and people like Jerome Wheeler were wiped out, victims of what would become the West's boom-or-bust legacy.

COLORADO

Ranching and potato farming became the valley's main industries, and there was barely enough of that to keep the town going. In the 1920s and 1930s, Aspen was a rotted shell. Many of its 700 or so residents were on relief, wasting their time drinking "crud" — a popular bourbon-and-milkshake drink — in the Jerome's now-seedy bar that doubled as an ice cream parlor.

Though only six hours from Denver, Aspen might as well have been on the moon. The once-grand Victorian homes could be bought for as little as $30. There were two grocery stores, but no doctor, no fire department, no laundry, no paved streets, no radio station and virtually no ambition among locals who saw no future.

The revival of the mid-Rockies region began in late 1941 when Pando, north of Leadville, was selected by the U.S. Army as the site for Camp Hale, which would be the training home of the 10th Mountain Division. To recharge after a brutal week of training, the schuss-happy soldiers would head over Independence Pass to ski down Aspen Mountain's one crudely built run, bunking at the Jerome for 25 cents a night and vowing to return if they lived through the war.

After the 10th left Camp Hale to fight the Germans in Italy, Aspen settled back into its doldrums until Walter Paepcke, the brilliant chairman of the Container Corporation of America, came to town during a leisurely tour in May 1945. After his wife, Elizabeth, declared her love for the mountains with their flowers and flocks of aspen trees, Paepcke — who called the valley his "sleeping beauty" — set out to turn this all-but-dead burg into a skiing and cultural mecca, an "Athens of the West" where America's captains of industry could replenish their bodies, as well as their minds.

The Paepckes returned that fall and set up the Aspen Company to restore the Jerome and many of the town's decaying Victorian homes. Paepcke also spent $250,000 on a three-mile-long chair lift on Aspen Mountain — a full-day ticket cost $3.75 — and in January 1947, the valley's ski industry was officially born.

By then, of course, World War II was over and members of the 10th had filtered back to Aspen to burn powder all day and carouse all night. One of their brightest lights was Friedl Pfeifer, a legendary European ski-racing champion who had come to America in 1936 to teach his sport at Sun Valley before joining the 10th.

Pfeifer's ski background dovetailed nicely with Paepcke's plans with the Aspen Skiing Company, and he designed more trails on Aspen Mountain and organized the Aspen Ski School. Paepcke also founded the Aspen Institute, persuading eminences like Albert Schweitzer and writer Thornton Wilder to come out to lecture in the mountains.

By the late 1950s, Paepcke had pumped more than $1 million into the community. In the meantime, "Whip" Jones built the Aspen Highlands ski area in the Maroon Creek Valley southwest of town in 1958. Pfeifer left the Aspen Skiing Company and built Buttermilk. Snowmass transformed the wild Brush Creek area when it opened in 1967, and since then, nothing in the Roaring Fork River Valley has been the same.

Today, homes sell for millions of dollars. There's a world-famous music festival every summer. London- and Paris-based shops have come to town. And the skiing keeps getting better. Indeed, these developments have apparently put to rest the curse the Ute Indians left behind when those ambitious miners drove them out of the valley.

"The white man will never prosper off this land as long as the grass grows and the water flows," the Utes declared.

Today, they wouldn't know the place. ⁂

COLORADO

COLORADO
Ski!

PHOTOGRAPHY BY DAVID LISSY

WESTCLIFFE PUBLISHERS, INC. ENGLEWOOD, COLORADO

CONTENTS

International Standard Book Number:
ISBN 0-942394-82-8
Library of Congress Catalogue Card Number:
88-050697
Photographs and Captions: Copyright 1988 David Lissy.
All Other Non-Archival Text: Copyright 1988 Westcliffe
Publishers, Inc. All Rights Reserved.
Editor: John Fielder
Assistant Editor: Margaret Terrell Morse
Production Manager: Mary Jo Lawrence
Typographer: Richard M. Kohen
Printed in Japan by Dai Nippon Printing Company, Ltd.
Publisher: Westcliffe Publishers, Inc.
        2650 South Zuni Street
        Englewood, Colorado 80110
No portion of this book, either photographs or text, may
be reproduced in any form without the written permission
of the publisher.

Westcliffe Publishers wishes to thank
Eastman Kodak Company for its
generous contribution to the
production of this book.

Bibliography, The 10th Mountain Division

We are grateful to the Western History Department of
the Denver Public Library, particularly Lisa Backman and
Augie Mastrogiuseppe, for their help in providing access
to the 10th Mountain Division Collection, including
photography of Camp Hale letterhead artwork from the
Ralph Hulbert Collection.

The source of each quotation is followed by the page
number in this book on which the quotation appears. All
materials cited are in the 10th Mountain Division Collection, Western History Department, Denver Public Library.

1. *Ski the High Trail*, Harris Dusenbery: 15, 19, 20, 22,
24, 26, 31, 33, 34, 40, 42, 43, 44, 49, 50, 53, 58, 62,
65, 70, 71, 72, 75, 76, 78, 81, 86, 88, 90, 91, 92, 97,
102, 108.

2. Letters from Ralph W. Hulbert to Mrs. C.P. Hulbert:
16, 51, 54, 55, 57, 69, 84, 100, 106, 111.

3. *Manual for Mountain Troops*, Mountain Training
Center, Camp Hale, Richard Over Collection: 28, 38, 94,
98, 104.

4. *Songs of the 10th Mountain Division*, Richard Over
Collection: 36, 60, 61, 82.

*Page 1: Tandem skiers cut up fresh powder on Buffalo Pass
that can be reached only with a lift from Steamboat Powder
Cats, Steamboat Springs*

*Pages 2-3: First tracks in Oly Bowl with the Maroon Bells in
the distance, Aspen Highlands*

*Page 4: Last rays of sunset illuminate a nordic pair striding
along a ridge, Arapahoe Basin*

Page 5: Sunrise paints the top of Mount Daley, Snowmass

*Right: Guenther Mader of Austria takes flight during the
World Cup Downhill, Beaver Creek*

FOREWORD

What attracts people to Colorado's ski slopes year after year? Ski racing brought me at first — the National Junior Championships in Winter Park and Aspen in 1958 and 1960. Throughout the 60s it was the U.S. Ski Team qualification races and the University of Colorado. But what convinced me to want to spend the rest of my life here was the skiing — the quality, the variety, the ideal combination of sunshine and powder snow.

What I like about skiing is that it makes you feel like a kid no matter what age you are. If you're a five-year-old kid, you probably like feeling the freedom. If you're a 75-year-old kid, you may ski Colorado just for the scenery. Skiing keeps you young because it gives you that same sense of discovery that kids have all the time.

What is a good age to start skiing? I was five when I began in Vermont; my kids were two when I started them in Steamboat. The youngest skier I've ever seen was the 11-month-old son of Steamboat's police chief. I skied a few hundred feet with him down a very gentle slope at the bottom of the mountain. When he stopped and

A family outing on a perfect winter day, Steamboat Springs

his father unhooked his bindings, the kid fell over and crawled away. Because his skis and boots held him up, he could literally ski before he could walk.

When you're five, you love skiing because you

can just jump on your skis and go. You're free! At 10 and 12 you can go even farther and faster.

If you're a teenager, you may be interested in ski racing. What's it like to race downhill in the Olympics? Whether you want the adrenalin rush or the glory, if you want to go for the gold, Colorado is the place to train.

In college, the social part of skiing is most important. If you're going for the gold in après skiing, you don't want to miss any of the training at Colorado's ski areas.

In your 20s and 30s, having kids means experiencing the joy of family skiing. It's not only fun for your kids and fun watching your kids, it's also a kick for you. Shared experiences bridge the generation gap and bring the family closer. And the stories you take home with you are as much fun as your days on the slopes.

At 40 or 50, you become selective about where

and when you ski. Once you've skied Colorado you get spoiled because it's about the best in the world, so you may not ski anywhere else. You may ski only on sunny days or on fresh powder days or, like the natives, only when there's both.

By 60 or 70, most people think about retirement and sitting around watching television. But you folks who ski have a great sense of youthfulness. Your exhilaration comes from finding new experiences on the trails and in the ski towns.

Several years ago a 68-year-old lady came to my racing camp in Steamboat. She had skied all her life and was looking for a new challenge. I said, "I have to warn you now, because you can get addicted to racing." She was in the camp for a week and got hooked. The next year she joined a racing team.

One of the great things about skiing is that you can choose your danger level to suit your personality. You can feel the adrenalin rush with the same intensity regardless of your ability or your age. A downhill racer's 80-mile-an-hour rush is felt by a beginner at five miles an hour and by an expert while screaming through the moguls. Some days you get lucky and ski really deep powder — waist-deep, chest-deep, chin-deep, snorkle days! You sink down, it's up in your face and you're in danger of freezing your teeth because of the big grin on your face.

Regardless of your age or ability or personality, I think the Rocky Mountains offer you the best skiing in the world. When you ski Colorado, whether it's your first time or your fiftieth, you'll probably want to take back more than just great memories. I recommend a cowboy hat and this book.

— BILLY KIDD
1964 Olympic Silver Medalist
1970 World Champion
Director of Skiing, Steamboat

9

PREFACE

The first time I ever skied in Colorado — back in the 1960s — I drove up from Denver on a day that didn't seem anything out of the ordinary. Yes, it was clear, but then clear skies are not unusual in Colorado. Heading into the mountains I noticed a light dusting of fresh snow on the side of the road, but since the road surface itself was dry, I didn't think much about it. It wasn't until I turned on the car radio and heard the snow report that I realized what I was heading for. A foot of snow had fallen at the central Colorado ski areas the night before, the wind was calm and the temperature was 25 degrees and rising.

Astonished and delighted at this news, I suddenly understood the disadvantage of driving a 1958 VW Beetle over 12,000-foot Loveland Pass (25 miles an hour was its top speed). But, boy did I go fast after I reached the summit and started down the other side! Pulling into the resort parking lot, I grabbed my gear and literally ran for the ticket window (as well as a person can run in ski boots).

Without consulting a trail map or asking anyone where I was going, I hopped onto the first chair lift I saw. At the top, without stopping to look at the view, I plunged into untracked powder. It was perfect — deep enough to swirl around my legs with each turn, light enough to leave rooster tails of sparkling crystals behind. I managed only two or three turns in succession before I fell, but the smile on my face was still wide enough to leave stretch marks. Off to my right I heard whooping; off to my left someone yodeled. At the bottom of the run, as I hung over my poles in blissful exhaustion (two parts altitude sickness, one part fatigue), I heard someone say, "This is so much fun, it must be illegal!"

That's one way to describe a good day of Colorado skiing. You could also call it exhilarating, stimulating, rewarding, challenging or all of the above. What makes Colorado so special for skiers? It's a combination of factors. Here are a few:

THE RIGHT WHITE. A desert-like climate combined with the mountains' weather-making characteristics produce the kind of snow that skiers love. Some of the ski towns stand at over 8,000 feet above sea level, and from there lifts may rise to over 11,000 feet. The result is cold temperatures, cold enough to produce snow from November to May, or even longer. Storms usually move eastward from the Pacific, gradually drying out as they dump moisture on successive mountain ranges. That means the snowfall is not only steady but dry. It's not unusual for the snowpack to be less than 6 percent water.

ABUNDANT SUNSHINE. No, it doesn't snow all the time in Colorado. The weather varies, just as it does everywhere. I've seen years when it snowed twice a week with astonishing regularity. I've seen other years when high-pressure systems hung over the entire Rocky Mountain region for weeks on end, bringing unrelieved fair weather.

One enduring myth claims that it snows in Colorado only at night, with bright sunshine every day. Though this is sometimes the pattern, the usual course of events is that it snows whenever the storms move in, and the sun returns when the storms move out. Generally, there is more sunshine and more snowfall in March and April than in January and February.

TERRIFIC TOPOGRAPHY. The Rockies are relatively young, as mountains go, with rugged, angular peaks rising out of flat, sage-covered mountain parks. Above treeline the mountains are often inhospitable in winter — cold and windy — but in the lower regions, combinations of ridges, gulches, steep faces, gentle meadows and open bowls make for an incredible variety of good skiing terrain. Best yet, each mountain has its own topographical personality.

Over the past 20 years I've had the opportunity to ski all the major areas in the Colorado Rockies, but when anyone asks me what my favorite mountain is, I answer with another question: Favorite for what? There's so much terrain, so many interesting combinations of ridges, gulches, glades and bowls that you can keep sampling the choices for years, picking new favorites as you go.

GOOD TOWNS. There is more to skiing than just sliding, of course. There is also the experience provided by the facilities at the base. Full-fledged ski towns support large year-round populations, ultramodern resorts cater strictly to visitors, refurbished mining towns retain the look of Victorian times, and still other areas defy all such labels.

But all Colorado's ski areas have one thing in common: given the right combination of sun and snow, you feel as though you never want to leave.

— BILL GROUT
Editor-in-Chief
SKIING Magazine

Late afternoon sun highlights moguls on Mary Jane's Golden Spike, Winter Park

The 10th Mountain Division

"If a camera could possibly show the wonder of such a spot I'd send you some pictures but it's hard even to believe one's eyes so no photograph could ever catch it."

The year was 1943. The location was the snowy slopes above Camp Hale, Colorado, the training ground of the U.S. Army's 10th Mountain Division. The writer — Sergeant Ralph Hulbert — was describing scenery he'd climbed thousands of vertical feet to witness. On his feet were seven-foot wooden skis; on his back was a 90-pound rucksack.

Forty-five years later I'm standing on a similar slope, but my skis are lightweight Fiberglas and my 60-pound pack contains cameras and film instead of a stove and sleeping bag. My mission is not to train for mountain combat against the Nazis, but to capture the wonder and the beauty of Colorado's ski country.

Like most of the men of the 10th Mountain Division, I was born east of the Mississippi River. I too was lured west by the Rocky Mountains. And like many "phantoms of the snow" who returned after the war ended, I decided to make Colorado my home. Even now, after 12 years of photographing in these mountains, I am still left with the empty feeling of not being able to put it all on film. It's simply too big, too wonderful, too beautiful. Surely the mountains reveal part of God's glory and nature to us.

Copyright 1988 Mike Meleski

To reach the slope where I now stand I did not strap "climbers" to my skis and sweat my way up like Ralph Hulbert and the other "soldiers of the snows." A chair lift carried me to this mountaintop, giving me time to think back on the early days of skiing in Colorado.

When Camp Hale was built in 1942, the industry was fledgling: single rope tows at Loveland and Berthoud, a rope tow and T-bar at Winter Park, a sled-like lift that had to be manually hauled up the hill at Aspen. When Camp Hale's mile-and-a-10th-long T-bar was built on Cooper Hill, it was the longest in the world.

The Army chose the Camp Hale site because of its 9,300-foot elevation, steep terrain, light powder snow and long, hard winters. A glamorous recruitment campaign brought Ivy League skiers, rugged outdoorsmen and even a few ski champions to the mountain valley. During the winters of 1942 to 1944, 14,000 soldiers learned and refined ski and outdoor survival techniques on Cooper Hill and in the backcountry above Camp Hale. During the "D" Series maneuvers, described by Harris Dusenbery in this book, the entire division took to the mountains for 30 days of mock warfare, fighting minus-30-degree temperatures as well as the "enemy," fellow soldiers posing as Germans.

The same qualities that drew the Army to Colorado brought thousands of 10th Mountain Division skiers back to its slopes after the war. Tenth Mountain veterans helped launch many of the state's ski areas, including Vail, Aspen, Buttermilk, Snowmass, Breckenridge, Arapahoe Basin and Loveland. These men, more than any other group, had a profound impact on Colorado's ski industry.

Three-dimensional artifacts from the 10th Mountain Division — including skis and poles, clothing, sleeping bags and food rations — are on permanent display at the Colorado Ski Museum in Vail and are periodically on display at the Colorado History Museum in Denver. Written materials — including those excerpted in this book — are housed at the Denver Public Library.

Private Harris Dusenbery, who is quoted extensively in this book, was 29 when he joined the 10th Mountain Division in September 1943. He trained as a rifleman at Camp Hale for eight months, then served in Italy's Northern Apennines until the war ended in 1945. Portions of his *Ski the High Trail* memoir were written while stationed at Camp Hale. Sergeant Ralph Hulbert, whose letters to his mother are excerpted in this book, was 22 when he arrived at Camp Hale in 1943. He taught skiing, glacier climbing and mountain climbing, then went overseas to fight the Nazis in the mountains of Italy.

Every American is indebted to the men of the 10th who fought in Italy to preserve our freedoms. To those who died for that cause and to those who returned to Colorado to build our great ski industry — my special thanks.

— DAVID LISSY

Backcountry skiers survey the terrain on the Continental Divide, Loveland Pass
Above: Etched in granite on this 10th Mountain Division monument atop Tennessee Pass are the names of the 990 men who died in Italy

13

"I stood facing toward snowy peaks and the pyramid that we called Ptarmigan Mountain. Behind me abruptly rose the shoulders and peak of Sugarloaf. Around me the distant horizon was encircled with jagged summits and snow-covered ridges, range after range of glorious mountains, all sparkling in the moonlight.

The world above timberline is a strange world, far different than the world that is the normal habitat of man. It is a land dominated by the wind, the snow and the great hard cruel rocks. It is a land of nature's outposts and feeble thrusts against the cold, silence and death of outer space. There nature, as we usually think of it, maintains a ceaseless struggle, advancing a little here and retreating in some other place, but always maintaining a precarious balance between the forces of life in nature and the maw of death in space. Along this borderline nature's hardiest species keep up a ceaseless struggle, holding the line against the intrusion of the forces of death into our world of growth and life. This land where

The Needles provide a dramatic backdrop for a group of nordic skiers, Purgatory

nature wanes has a beauty all its own, and in its beauty and in its lifelessness it offers a challenge to any living creature. There the weather

CAMP HALE

COLORADO

is foe to man, beast and tree. With majestic impartiality space makes its death demand of all, and sturdy must be he who would resist the tide-like sweep of all life into its everlasting stillness. This frontier between life and death is truly a hell-land as well as a wonderland.

The wind whistled softly about my parka hood and blew whirling wisps of snow along the surface. I knew that this was a perfect spring night at twelve thousand feet of elevation in the Colorado Rockies.

I glanced at the mountains ahead and then turned my head to the snow dome behind me. I carefully scanned the slopes below. I saw nothing, nothing that did not belong in the scene, neither man nor sign of man. I felt perfectly alone, in the center of vast ranges of mountains. The wind seemed only to emphasize the stillness of the night and the majesty of the region.

For some reason I glanced down to the snow surface I was standing on, and there among some rocks that lay but a few feet to my left were some tracks. I was startled for an instant. What creature could have made them? They were not man-

made. I examined them more carefully and found them to be the prints of small hoofs. They must be, I thought, the tracks of Rocky Mountain sheep, but I had not seen any in my months in the mountains around Camp Hale.

What kind of creature is this that dwells in this above-nature region? What similarity has this creature to man that sends it up into regions where man penetrates for adventure or is at times forced to go by the Army? This mountain sheep may be up here to avoid enemies more cruel than the cold and the wind. They could be a pack of voracious wolves. A terrible pack imbued with far more greed and cruelty, a pack of my own kind, is my reason for being on this spot at this time.

Why the tracks of that mountain sheep should deeply impress me I do not know, but they did and thereupon became a part of me, never to be forgotten. That sheep was perhaps there for the same purpose that I was. It looked upon the same scene. It sniffed of the same wind. Our trails only crossed and the mountain sheep had gone its way and I was to go mine."

15

Tracks left behind by a couple of powder hounds, Loveland Basin

Huge granite outcropping makes a perfect launchpad for this member of Colorado's air force, Spaulding Bowl, Copper Mountain

21 April 1943, Camp Hale
"We climbed for about four hours....When we finally reached the top we were up about 13,000 feet with 1,500 feet of vertical descent to occupy us during the next hour. Wow, what a time!"

*S*unset illuminates Mount Werner and
an old barn, Steamboat Springs

"This view was the last that I had of the
works of civilized or peacefully constructive
mankind. All that lay ahead of us was the
Army and nature, a few days of work and
suffering, and we would be back in a rest
area. Our only real enemy would be twelve
thousand feet of elevation, but at times that
can be mean enough for any man."

*S wiss racer Luc Genolet approaches speeds of 80 m.p.h. as he
hurtles down the World Championship Centennial Course,
Beaver Creek*

*Clouds shroud Red Mountain as a skier heads down Aztec
at the America's Downhill, Aspen*

"As the column went on and on the Divide seemed to
be retreating from us, but on looking around I could
see far down across the expanse of sparkling snow the
now insignificant-appearing saddle from which we had
started this traverse."

$\mathcal{D}$arkness settles over a sparkling Victorian scene, Telluride

Dropping off See Forever onto the mountain's steep face, Telluride

"We plunged into thickets of spruce and fought our
way through aspen. We glided easily and silently
across open spaces. We heard and saw nothing.
We did little talking."

24 *Friends explore fresh powder down Dragon's Teeth in China Bowl, Vail*

"We stopped for a breather and looked around. With the moon and the stars overhead and the snow underfoot we were alone in the universe. After resting for a minute or two and once again breathing more easily, I remarked to the man in front of me,

'Wouldn't this make a ski hill?'

'Yah. But you need a tow. Put a ski tow up here and you could really have fun,' he replied."

Fairfield Resort's Nordic Center treats skiers to miles of groomed trails, Pagosa Springs

Dramatic display of frost coats aspen trees on Buttermilk Mountain, Aspen

"The knot of men unwound into a column of silently moving shadows, and began angling up and over the shoulder to our right. The whole patrol was clad in camouflage whites, but the half moon cast black shadows against the sparkling snow."

*T*ad Langlois soars off the 90-meter jump at Howelson Hill during the U.S. Nationals, Steamboat Springs

Watch out below: Hiroko Fugii of Japan performs a back layout at the Freestyle World Cup, Breckenridge

1 October 1943, Camp Hale: "Eventually the mountain soldier must learn to ski without falling. Falling causes fatigue, injury, and loss of time. But since it is impossible to learn to ski without falling often, the soldier should also learn how to fall in the manner that will best avoid injury."

Sunset colors the sky pink above the Continental Divide, Arapahoe Basin

"We could only test ourselves on the slope. Traverse and kick-turn, traverse and kick-turn, repeat and repeat it, herringbone up this slope, traverse again, side-step up this icy spot, rest, oh, so rarely did we rest, sweat and struggle on, gulp hard at the thin life-giving air, strain to keep up, utter a hundred vain curses for the fifty pounds of rucksack on your back, for the ache in your shoulders, the sweat in your eyes, the skis on your feet, but 'keep moving' is the order of the day."

A Run Down into the Unknown

"One after another the men in the column ahead of me disappeared down that first sharp drop from the cornice. I felt that universal nerve tingling that the skier always has before a run down into the unknown. I took a few steps forward and gravity took hold of me with its giant hand. It pulled me down in that first breathtaking drop. The great mysterious power of gravity never ceases to amaze me.

After the first steep drop we angled off in a traverse to control our speed. My squad stopped and checked our number. We had lost no one on the steep slope. Then away we went for another run.

It did not take us long to get down to the highest trees. There we found our advance squads waiting for us. They reported finding no sign of the enemy. The now united patrol was reorganized, and we skied on in single file. The slopes were becoming less steep, and the breakable crust of the higher ridges changed to powder. The trees were spruce, black and dense in

the moonlight, but they only grew in patches at this elevation, giving plenty of space for skiing.

This world of ours offers nothing surpassing

CAMP HALE, *COLORADO*

in beauty of form and texture those mountain spruce and brilliant snows that absorb all moonlight and reflect it all into the eyes of the awestruck beholder. See the innumerable shapes of tree and shadow, the ever-changing contour of bejeweled snow surfaces, the towering white ramparts of the Rockies on all sides, the star-filled sky overhead as brilliant as we have ever seen it with the half moon still shining, as it now was over Sugarloaf. As we went on, the patches of trees became long rows, and we sped down broad galleries that were sparklingly beautiful in the moonlight.

Farther down we entered a particularly heavy growth of trees, and the Captain gave us a break. Three of us, chosen because we did not smoke, were posted as sentries, and the rest of the men entered the thicket for a cigarette. . . .

The patrol was called together and the descent was resumed. We immediately ran into some difficult terrain that was quite steep and wooded. It required making short, precipitous runs and then stopping or turning abruptly in the soft snow. Many of us fell going through this stretch

of woods. I took one tumble that plunged me head first into soft snow under two large trees. I was carrying a rucksack and had my rifle slung over my shoulder. I lost my balance and the momentum of my pack and rifle threw me into the tree well. In such circumstances it is impossible to get back on one's feet without removing pack and rifle and possibly skis without the assistance of another man. Fortunately a man was able to stop right behind me. I was lucky he did not pile right in on top of me. He was a good skier. He reached out with his ski pole and I grasped it just above the ring. By leaning well back and heaving mightily he managed to pull me up, though the angle of tension was acute as I was lying downhill from him and the two spruce were on the other side. Atop my skis, I thanked him, shook the snow out of my mittens and was on my way within a minute."

33

Can't wait to drop down for another run from Colorado Heli-Ski's high-speed lift, Breckenridge

*H*eading for the finish on the World Championship
Centennial Course, Beaver Creek

No friends on a powder day: lone skier enjoys China Bowl, Vail

"Our view of the terrain from the Divide had shown
that we had 'one hell of a lot of ground to cover'...as
we were now discovering. The valley continued to
flatten out and become more open."

*C*hristmas visitors can enjoy an evening of ice skating
or night skiing, Keystone

*Waist deep in powder accessible only by a Steamboat Powder Cat,
Buffalo Pass*

"White clad G.I. Joe —
    We're the phantoms of the snow,
On our ski boards we're the mountain infantry.
    Happy go lucky free."

Late afternoon view from Berthoud Pass, Continental Divide

1 October 1943, Camp Hale: "In the previous war forty percent of the total casualties in the mountain troops of the warring nations were due to avalanches. To prevent such needless casualties every soldier who ventures onto steep snow slopes must be capable of telling when avalanche dangers exist."

*Jumping Jupiter Jones demonstrates a powder takeoff on the
varied terrain of Buffalo Pass, Steamboat Springs*

*Billy Kidd displays his medal-winning technique for
a crowd, Steamboat Springs*

*"We did everything but sleep with our skis fastened to
our feet and I suppose we would have done that at
times if we could have figured out some way to get the
skis inside our sleeping bags."*

*P*owder explosion, Loveland Basin

"*Looking back in the distance I could see the pass over which we had come. It rose so high and so very far away, and yet we had been there a scant two hours before....*

Family picnickers soak in the spring sunshine, Arapahoe Basin

*"...On either side of us the long sparkling white ridges
rose up and up to the shining summits of the Divide."*

44 *Fireworks light up the Winternational World Cup celebration, Aspen*

"At last we were able to build our fire....We took off our skis and sat down in the open end of our shelter facing the fire to bask in its lovely heat. This was our first chance to sit down in comfort."

Popping off the Ridge of Bell, Aspen

Last run of the day down Coonskin, Telluride

47

A High Rocky Bluff

"Our squad leader gave the order to move out, and we picked our way carefully up among the aspen. This type of skiing is no fun; it is just plain hard work. The slope had not become at all steep, as we were still on the alluvial fan, but every few yards the column stopped and we waited for long minutes. We had no idea what was happening ahead, but whatever it was we knew we would not like it. We heard no firing, so we felt sure that the advance elements were not deploying to take out opposition. Besides, it just never happened this early in a problem. In the crisp morning air only the swish of sliding skis and the occasional low voice of a man could be heard. The going must be tough up ahead. Our conversation was confined to bitching about this situation because we knew that before long we would be racing to catch up.

After a half hour of this I reached a point where I could see through the trees the cause for the delay: a high rocky bluff. The slope was very steep; the snow surface had turned to ice

and was cut up by rocky outcrops thrusting through the snow.

'It isn't a slope for skis,' I said to myself as I

CAMP HALE, *COLORADO*

contemplated the prospect. 'We should have crampons for this deal.'

But men on skis were disappearing over the top; it could be made. The battalion was going up in two columns and moving slowly. As my turn came I started up with an anxious glance at my worn climber. With the load on my back, a forty-pound rucksack and a ten-pound rifle, the ascent was work, hard work, nerve-wracking work. Edging my skis into the icy slope to keep from sliding down the steep slope was tiring on my ankles. Though I made my way upward slowly, I had to stop frequently to get my breath, as did the men around me. With the exertion that the slope required, a man's system craves oxygen, and the thin, cold air of that ten thousand foot elevation felt like a mighty poor substitute.

About halfway up the precipitous slope I suddenly felt my right ski slip back a few inches, but I managed to keep my balance. With a sinking feeling in my stomach I knew without looking down that my climber had finally broken. I took a few more steps with difficulty, hesitated

for a moment, and then pulled out of line to let the men behind me pass. I did a precarious balancing feat and removed my skis without taking off my pack or rifle. They would have slid down the icy slope if I had set them down. I put my skis and poles over my left shoulder and started climbing on foot. It was difficult to get footing with my mountain boots. Climbing that icy slope was more difficult than I anticipated. I slipped a few times but I had one free hand and could grasp an occasional aspen or rock protruding through the icy surface. I got to the top of this steep stretch with all my equipment about even with my place in the formation.

Just as soon as I gained the top of the rocky bluff the snow turned soft, and I sank up to my knees in the fluffy stuff. It was a change we so often encountered in the mountains, an abrupt change from a sunny icy slope to a forest's shade....

The column kept moving on, and I was not conscious of anyone paying the least attention to me. My plight was obvious but there was nothing they could do to help me. In a few minutes I succeeded in putting on the front half of the climber and fastened it at the toe-iron. I now had half a climber. It looked like it would work for uphill work. It would be awkward, but it might get me to that unknown destination high up in the shining mountains."

49

*E*vidence of cutting the Dragon's Teeth in China Bowl, Vail

"This was good skiing country. The long white slopes
ran down from the austere, windswept summits. There
would be good running here through powder snow
even in April. Spring had not yet come to the
mountains."

*Reaching for the sky with the Ten Mile Range below,
Spaulding Bowl, Copper Mountain*

26 March 1943, Camp Hale
*"Been issued lots more equipment — more still to
come too — and it sure is wonderful stuff. The only
complaint was that the only size of heavy socks
available was 13 — I use mine for sleeping bags!"*

"We were isolated and alone in time and
place, separated by the torturous
mountains from the mainstream of life.
Up there the tenuity of life was all too
apparent. What a thin slice life really is!
It is only a few miles from the molten hot
lavas under the ground to the lifeless cold
of the stratosphere."

*W*inter twilight, Purgatory

11 January 1945, Italy
"Until such information has been officially released I can't tell you where we are but I hope the censor will not mind a little description of our immediate surroundings....

*M*ount Crested Butte oversees another winter
afternoon, Crested Butte

*"...The mountains themselves look very much like
those we knew in Colorado but of course they're not as
high. They differ from our mountains in that
they are threaded with numerous roads and
contain many small villages."*

*Jetting down the
North Face,
Crested Butte*

57

21 April 1943, Camp Hale
"Spent the weekend skiing on slopes that
were about as wonderful for skiing as
anything I _ever_ saw in the movies....And
the view was unbelievable, 14,000 + ft.
mountains _all_ around us."

Young couple springs down Diamond Back en route to North Peak, Keystone

Set track enthusiasts, Telluride Nordic Center

"The sun came out on our slope and it began to get quite warm for the exertion that we were putting out. From an open spot I could look back and see Camp Hale far down in the valley...a pretty sight lying in the snow-covered valley."

Blasting through fresh powder down Steeplechase, Aspen Highlands

"The years may have more than one season
    But I can remember but one,
The time when the rivers are freezin'
    And the mountains with whiteness are spun,
The snowflakes are falling so fast,
    And the winter has come now at last....

More than a mouthful on Peak 8, Breckenridge

"...Two boards upon cold powder snow, YO HO!
What else does a man need to know?
Two boards upon cold powder snow, YO HO!
That's all that a man needs to know."

*Snow forms resemble
human shapes,
Snowmass*

"We were intruders into a void world high
on the mountain in the storm. We were
without women in being or in mind. As
such were we still men in the masculine
sense of the term? Had we not lost our
manhood to the cold, the snow and the
twelve thousand foot elevation?"

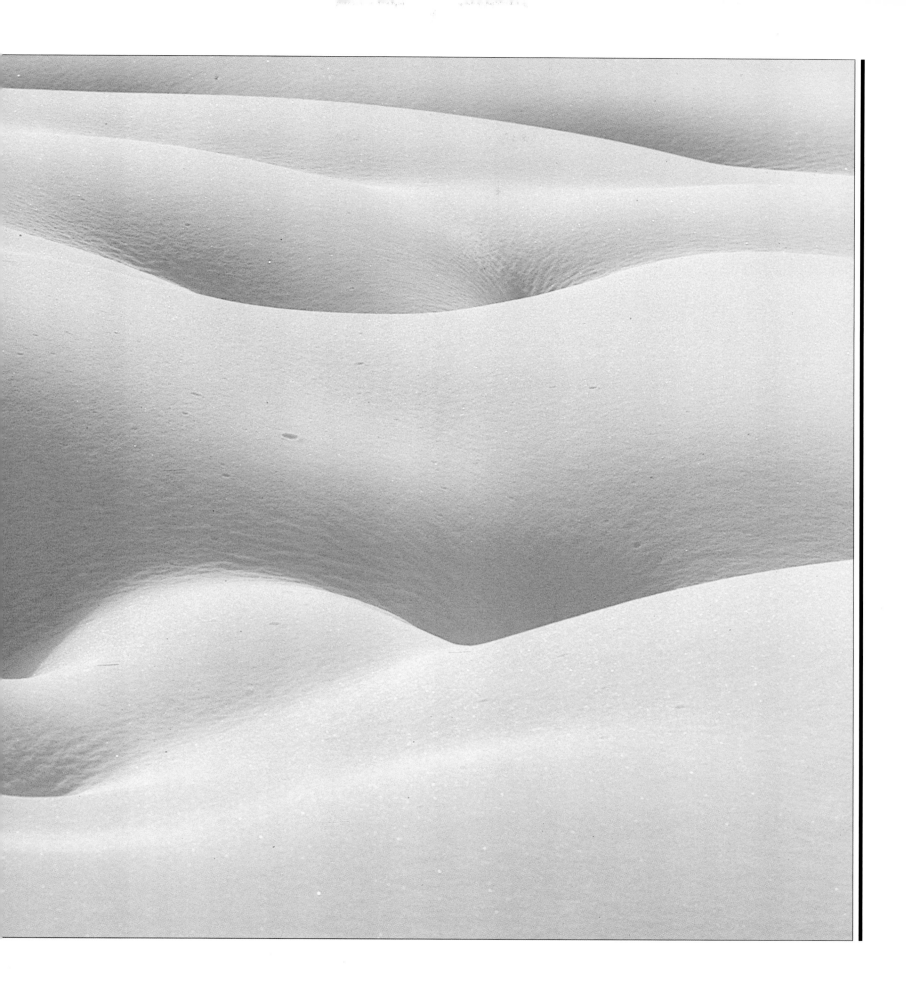

The Execution of the Order

"A Lieutenant came up to me and asked, 'Did you see the Major ski off in that direction?' He indicated the direction with a slight toss of a ski pole.

'Yes, I did,' I answered, as I had seen him ski off some minutes before.

'Well I have this message for him. He is over at the C.P. [Command Post]. It is right over there among some rocks. Just go out in the direction the Major went and you'll run into it. Here's the message.'

'Yes sir,' I answered in soldierly fashion. I stuffed the message into my parka pocket and skied off after the Major.

Apparently the Lieutenant had not known exactly where the C.P. was located and I certainly did not, although I vaguely remembered some rocks from earlier in the morning when visibility was better. I did not question how or why. I proceeded with the execution of the order instantly and habitually.

Perhaps I could find the Major's ski tracks

and follow them. After weaving for a bit on the outrun, I could not locate them. The snow was falling so fast it had already covered them, and

CAMP HALE, *COLORADO*

so my best hope was lost at the start.

I skied out boldly, boldly that is under the circumstances, and went over the rim of the pass and for perhaps a hundred yards down the far side. I had to ski carefully because the flat-lighting was terrific. It is disconcerting to ski under those conditions, knowing that what you see of the snow surface right down at your ski tips and on out to the limit of visibility is not what is actually there. You realize that at any moment you may drop into a deep hole or run right up against a snow bank. It is worse than skiing on the darkest night....

As my first move I made a ninety degree turn to my right and traversed out for about fifty yards. I saw nothing in the swirling snow on this steep part of the ridge. I did a kick-turn and came back. I started out to the left on the opposite traverse, but after getting out fifteen yards, I felt sure that this was not the direction and went back. Next I went out in my original direction for some fifty yards and found the slope had decreased considerably. I skied out to the left, saw nothing but flat-lighting and came back.

A lull in the storm allowed me a glimpse of a few snow-mantled spruce still farther out. I reasoned that the C.P. would not be in the trees because the Lieutenant had not mentioned them. It must be off somewhere to my right....I headed back up the ridge at an angle of one hundred and twenty degrees from my original course....By now my first ski tracks were undoubtedly covered by the heavy snow fall, but I felt sure of my location and of the direction back to my company area. My courses and runs, every move I had made, were mapped in my memory.

After regaining the elevation of the Pass but at a spot a couple of hundred yards from my starting point, I ran into a squad of men. I asked, but they had no idea where the C.P. was. I skied on, cutting to my left looking for rocks that might indicate the C.P. Some rocks appeared here and there, and then I came upon a gully a good twenty feet deep with a steep cornice on the west side....I started skiing down the gully and met a lone skier. He said that he too was looking for the C.P. We went on in opposite directions."

U.S.A. downhiller Tracey McEwan kicks out of the start house at the Winternational World Cup, Aspen

A triumphant Pam Fletcher shows her enthusiasm for winning the World Cup Downhill, as former President Gerald Ford looks on, Vail

67

 reparing for a soft landing in high-altitude powder, Arapahoe Basin

69

11 April 1943, Camp Hale
"Today I have been skiing since 9:30 this morning and had a simply super time. We have an area called Cooper Hill that has a mile and a tenth long lift on it and simply wonderful skiing. (6 inches of new powder fell last night!) Using seven foot skis, which are almost six inches longer than my own, and had a little trouble getting used to them."

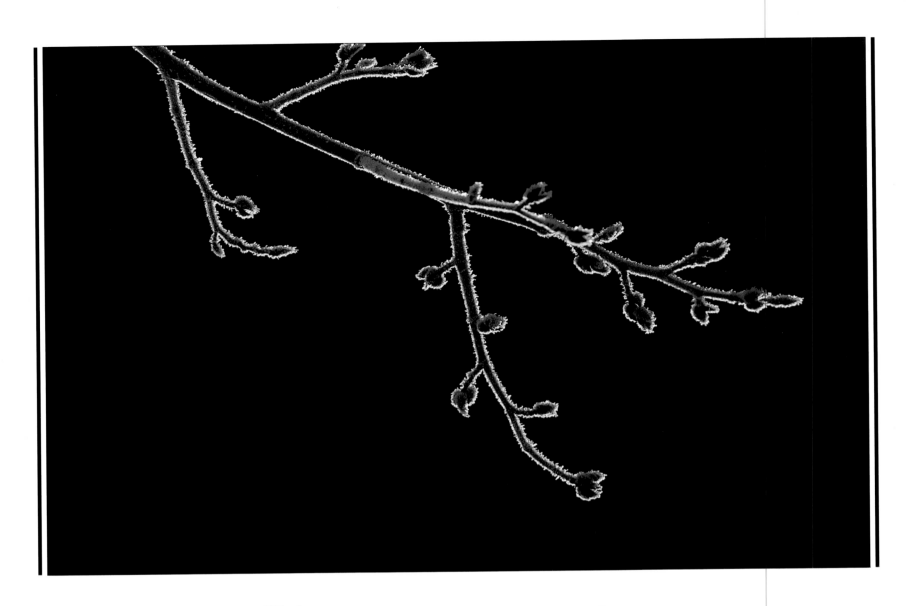

*F*rosted aspen buds are a sure sign that spring is just
around the corner, Aspen

"The moon hung lower in the western sky, but its rays
still reached down into the valley and cast shadows
black and sharp against the glistening snow."

*Hoar-frosted willows stand tall as morning's light burns off
frozen moisture, Telluride*

*"...it must have been the ghostly tree-shapes that took
my memories back so far. Few things can stir the
imagination like a night ride through country in which
there are pines and cedars of varying shapes and
with a contrasting background."*

*T*he East Wall looms behind this pair, Arapahoe Basin

Concentrating on negotiating the North Face, views often go unnoticed, Crested Butte

"Toward the latter part of the afternoon the trees began to thin out along the ridge....The sun was just above the western peaks and long black shadows of the men stretched out across the snow field."

An *eruption of snow crystals fills the*
air behind a bump masher
on Mary Jane's Golden Spike,
Winter Park

75

"Suddenly a skier loomed up out of the
blinding white pall of falling snow on the
edge of the cornice, which was a good
twenty feet high. He was skiing right for
the edge. I knew his danger from flat
lighting. I yelled 'Cornice' as loud as I
could and tried to motion him back. Good.
He stopped and turned back. I skied on."

A *foursome finds fresh powder off Peak 8, Breckenridge*

Floating into the valley between Peaks 8 and 9, Breckenridge

"It had been a warm day, but now the first chill of
evening was in the air. I was not happy to realize that
with evening upon us we were perhaps a long way
from our objective. I had hoped that the battalion
would turn down and bivouac in the highest groves of
evergreens along Pearl Creek."

*M*ount Wilson glows in soft morning light, Telluride

*Aspen branch bends under the weight of freshly fallen snow
on the Roaring Fork River, Aspen*

*"I raised my eyes to the view that stretched out before
me, range after range of mountains, dazzling white
peaks and long ridges....The majestic beauty of these
ranges made me realize that there were some
compensations for being in the mountain troops."*

The Microcosm of Man

" 'What time is it?' I asked generally.

'It's three o'clock,' someone replied out of the darkness.

'You men in Squads One and Two fix your beds,' ordered the Captain. 'The rest of us will organize our security for the night.' . . .

The lucky men in Squads One and Two made their beds and settled down; the patrols slipped away into the blackness of the night. It was much darker now that the moon had gone down behind the west range of snow-capped peaks, but those peaks still stood out in sharp relief against the starlit night. From down among the aspen and willows of the creek bottom we looked up to the mountains, majestic and aloof, far removed from us in the unitary stream of time and space, yet the breadth of that stream had been measured by us in fatigue and weariness.

Sometime later the Captain and the Staff Sergeant came up to me and suggested that I go with them. We took up a position just across the creek from the camp site and above it on

the bank that lay between the creek and the highway. We were not more than thirty yards from the sleeping men and we had a good view

of the whole area. At this spot there was good concealment in the trees, so the Captain suggested that we stay here.

Under a pine tree large for that high elevation we found a space free from snow on a slope of thirty degrees. Here we prepared to 'sweat out' the next two hours. We took off our skis and seated ourselves upon the frozen ground. I laid my rifle down close at hand. This was the first time in twenty hours that I had taken off my skis except for a few minutes back in our battalion area. The unencumbered feeling was strange and it took me some minutes to get used to it. For minutes afterwards my feet felt as though the skis were still securely attached.

We sat there on the frozen ground of the bank and talked briefly and intermittently on a variety of subjects. There was not much to say. The past was too remote, the present was too insignificant and at the same time so overpowering, and the future was too uncertain. We were strangers with all of the present in common and nothing of the past to compare with it. What we had in common seemed at the time to be not worth talking about.

Within ten minutes I could feel the cold begin to penetrate my clothing, well armored as I was against the cold. I wore wool underwear, two pair of arctic wool socks, double wool ski pants, a wool shirt, a wool sweater and a heavy double canvas parka. A ski cap, two pair of mittens, one wool and one canvas, and ski boots, which are not the warmest type of footwear, completed my protection against the cold. I was sleepy and tired and hungry, but these are small discomforts. There was the awful cold, and it at times can really hurt.

The Staff Sergeant got up, stamped his feet, and swung his arms about to increase the circulation of blood. I followed suit. The Captain finally gave in, and he too stood up and stamped around. For long stretches our conversation sank into complete silence. We were suffering, yet we were too tired to do anything about it. We would sit down for a few minutes, and then when we got too cold, we stood up. The night was lasting forever. Wait. Wait. Wait. Time was standing still. Not quite, two more minutes had passed in their long trek to eternity. Standing there with nothing to do but watch time pass, I felt the microcosm of man and his infinite subordination to time and space."

82 *A windswept mountaintop and the Resolution run challenge this group of heli skiers, Ten Mile Range*

"Men of steel and sons of Mars,
    Under freedom's stripes and stars —
We are ski men — we are free men
    And mountains are our home.

Sling your packs and mount your skis
    Stem the slopes through rocks
    and trees —
Let echoes ring with the song we sing
    Snap out the cadence with your
    rifle sling."

A snowy afternoon on the mall, Beaver Creek

Snow falls lightly as skiers head for the slopes, Vail

11 January 1945, Italy
*"These towns are all made of stone and are quite snug
and picturesque. They and their folk have seen much
war however. I hope our passage through will bring
them the peace that they seem to embody."*

*S*igrid Wolf negotiates a turn through a blinding snow squall on the
America's Downhill course, Aspen

Yahoo! Blue sky, fresh powder and another satisfied customer, Aspen

*"There before us was the tremendous ever-steepening
curve of the mountain, and within us we felt the
steadily falling curve of our available energy."*

*D*eep snowpack on the
Ruby Mountains,
Crested Butte

"Here was only the star-lit night and the
penetrating cold, seemingly the cold of
outer space from beyond the ken of man.
The earth had given up her warmth and
was giving up her life to the surrounding
void of eternal and ravenous cold,
insatiable until it has taken all."

S ky and snow blend together in an eerie scene in Parsenn Bowl, Winter Park

"With the coming of full daylight it began to snow harder. A combination of fog with the swirling snow reduced visibility to a few yards....

First one to the bottom gets the front seat on Colorado's fastest ski lift, Ten Mile Range

"...In addition there was flat lighting also called a white out, that peculiar phenomenon in snow country making every snow surface appear perfectly flat and on the same plane with every other snow surface."

*B*ump runs offer skiers of all abilities plenty of challenges;
this one on Highline, Vail

This much fun ought to be illegal, Peak 8, Breckenridge

*"At the time for the next break...we talked in low tones
of what a nice ski run we would have had if it had not
been for all our equipment."*

*N*ordic skier enjoys a trail past a log cabin at the Nordic Ski Center, Breckenridge

1 October 1943, Camp Hale: "Walking on the level...is the simplest movement in skiing. The arms and legs move as in marching on the level, except that the feet and skis are not lifted off the snow, but slide forward in a gliding motion. If the weight of the skis is lifted by the leg muscles every time a step is taken, the many thousands of steps taken during the day's march will result in early fatigue. Let the snow carry the weight of the ski."

The Enemy

"I tossed the [C ration] can away, scrambled for my rifle, slung it across my shoulders, put on my mittens, grabbed my ski poles and took off after the rest of the patrol that was heading up the bank and into the woods. I could now see several of the enemy across the creek and up on the highway. There was a desultory firing of blanks. Someone in the enemy ranks shouted, 'Stop. We've got you covered with machine guns.' I was the last man. I kept on going.

Our patrol was in peril. We paid no attention to the shouting and the firing and kept right on forging ahead. My breath came hard. I was bitter. I recognized that the situation was disastrous. It was a complete snafu. If it had occurred in combat, we would all have been 'dead ducks' as the men in our outfit put it.

Apparently the enemy had been as surprised at the encounter as we had been, but they quickly sent out skiers after us. I saw them come sweeping down the far slope from the highway like hawks on their prey, we in white, they in green.

I was out of breath from climbing a steep bank up which I had to break trail, having taken what I thought was a short-cut. The snow was soft

CAMP HALE, *COLORADO*

and heavy. It would have been faster for me and much less work to have followed in the trail of the others who got a head start, but that trail led around closer to the enemy and instinct forced me to take the short-cut up over the fresh snow. I knew that I could not go faster than the rest of the patrol. On top of the first steep bank I reached their track heading up into the woods and followed it. My only chance, I thought, now that I was behind was to keep in the packed trail. I could not hope to elude my pursuers by breaking to the side and hiding in the bush because of the trail I would leave. I entered the woods feeling that the enemy skiers were fairly close, but I could not see any except for a few still over on the highway. I felt a certain resentment that we had not left our vulnerable position earlier in the morning.

It is a common human failing particularly in times of emotional stress to form opinions on the basis of insufficient facts. I had been asleep between the hours of six and nine, and I knew absolutely nothing of what went on during that time. I acquired no knowledge after getting up; I

was too busy with breakfast. Under the circumstances I had no right to feel critical of our leadership, but the emotion was there nonetheless. I could not express my feelings at the moment and I was too busy besides. Under the stress of circumstances I did not analyze my feelings, I merely felt them. . . .

I plowed ahead through the soft snow as fast as I could. Even with the trail it was hard grueling work and I could already feel the sweat on my face. Apparently some of the enemy skiers entered the woods from a converging direction. I did not realize my pursuers were near until a man swooped upon me from behind, grasped my rifle which was slung across my back and hurled me to the snow. As I went down I saw the last man in our patrol disappear over a rise and into the woods some twenty yards ahead."

Views of the Gore Range and Lake Dillon from North Peak highlight this powder run, Keystone

Plenty of airtime can be found off the North Rim's cliffs and rocks, Vail

1 October 1943, Camp Hale: "The stem christiania is the most advanced turn to be learned by the soldier. It is a good turn in both soft snow and hard snow, on steep or gradual slopes, and can be used at moderate speed or high speed."

$\mathcal{P}$eak 8 basks in sunrise's golden splendor, Breckenridge

22 February 1945, Italy
"We've had a bit of good luck during the last few days and now find ourselves with quite a reputation as mountaineers. Our operation was a complete success in every way — especially since the German SS troops maintained it was absolutely impossible to attack where we did!"

Couloir just below the summit of Red Mountain Pass, Silverton

The Pine Cliffs at Mary Jane provide many challenges, not the least of which is keeping both skis on the ground, Winter Park

"At twelve thousand feet you...feel that all life lies below you, and above, above you is nothing but the awful void of space, so empty, so cold, so quiet."

104

Backcountry traveler climbs up a steep rock face to reach some of Colorado's steepest and deepest, Silverton

1 October 1943, Camp Hale: "The mountain soldier who has learned his fundamentals in the ski school must learn to ski with a pack and rifle before putting the fundamentals into practice in the mountains....Skiing with a pack and rifle on steep slopes, narrow paths, soft snow, hard snow, breakable crust, etc., will present difficulties for which the mountain soldier must be prepared."

A *break during a winter snowstorm offers sunshine and fresh powder at Hanging Valley, Snowmass*

Nothing to frown about on a day like this, Breckenridge

2 May 1943, Camp Hale
"We climbed & ran the ridge three or four times together. The skiing was perfect, nothing less. And we __had__ to ski all the time 'cause as soon as you stepped off your boards you were shoulder deep in soft spring snow."

Just before dawn, Aspen

*Mount Crested Butte rises spectacularly
above the Silver Queen lift, Crested Butte*

"*The birth of a new day is one morning, here and
everywhere: above the clouds where the sun shines
clear, here on this snow swept pass, and far down in
the valley where this same weather is pouring rain.*"

H̶igh above it all you can "See Forever," Telluride

2 May 1943, Camp Hale
"...from the top of the ridge it looked as if the whole of the Rocky Mountain Range was around us. Nothing but snow clad rugged peaks around and no other people for miles. If a camera could possibly show the wonder of such a spot I'd send you some pictures but it's hard even to believe one's eyes so no photograph could ever catch it."

ACKNOWLEDGEMENTS

A special dedication goes to all the "phantoms of the snow," the men of the 10th Mountain Division, who fought and died defending our freedom.

Thanks to the following ski resorts and services, who helped coordinate my photography plans at their areas: Aspen Highlands, Aspen Skiing Company, Breckenridge, Breckenridge Nordic Ski Center, Colorado Heli-Ski, Copper Mountain Resort, Crested Butte, Fairfield Pagosa Resort, Keystone/Arapahoe Basin, Loveland Basin, Purgatory, Steamboat Powder Cats, Steamboat Ski Corporation, Telluride, Tenth Mountain Trail Association, Vail/Beaver Creek, Winter Park Resort and Wolf Creek.

Thanks to the following companies who provided equipment, clothing and film: Bollé; Descente; Dynastar, Inc.; Eastman Kodak Company; Fila Sports, Inc.; K-2 Corp.; Marker Ski Bindings; Obermeyer; Patagonia, Inc.; Roffe, Inc.; Rossignol; Salomon/North America, Inc.; Scott, USA; Tabar, Inc.; and White Stag.

Models who contributed their time and talent to this book include: Kevin Alexander, Mark Alt, Amy Atkins, Pat Berka, Brian Bonehake, Lars D. Carlson, Jennifer L. Cook, Rich Coulombe, Bob Curvey, Therese E.D. Dayton, John R. Dickinson, Peter Englehardt, the Fielder family, Dan Finholm, Tony Forrest, Shelley Garcia, Deborah Hartvigsen, Karin Henszey, Julie Hoff, Susan C. James, Jupiter Jones, Judy Kehin, Scott Kennett, Bill Kerig, the Lissy family, Tawnia McEves, Cathy McNice, Jim Middleton, Pat Mitchell, Debra Moore, Jerry Page, Gary Pesso, Kirk Rawles, Scott Rawles, Dick Reilly, Brian Rickauer, Eric Scharmer, Denise Silfven, Lisa M. Skube, Tom Stillo, the White family and Diane Young.

Technical Information

The photographs in this book were made with Nikon F-2 and F-3 camera bodies with MD-2 and MD-4 motor drives. Nikon lenses used included 16mm, 28mm, 35mm, 105mm, 180mm, 300mm and an 80–200mm zoom. Bronica ETR bodies were also used. Lenses used included 40mm, 75mm and 150mm. All photographs were made using Kodachrome 25 and 64 professional films. Shutter speeds ranged from 20 seconds to 1/60 second for the night shots and the scenics; speeds of 1/500 second and 1/1,000 second were used for the action shots. Aperture settings ranged from f/2.8 to f/16. No filtration was used on any of the photographs.

— D.L.

A pair of adventurers cling to a slope at sunset, Arapahoe Basin